SMPLE-KOIN

A BUDDHIST CRYPTOCURRENCY OPTIMISED FOR
MATERIAL SUFFICIENCY WITHIN GAME THEORY DYNAMICS

Samuel Alexander

SMPLE-KOIN: A Buddhist Cryptocurrency Optimised for Material Sufficiency within Game Theory Dynamics
ISBN: 978-1-7641411-4-7
Copyright 2025 © Samuel Alexander
Creative Commons (Non-Commercial)
Published by the Simplicity Institute 2025
Cover design by Andrew Doodson, Copyright © 2025

Acknowledgements:
Thanks to Bhikkhu Jinasiri and Josh Floyd for sharing astute feedback on the manuscript. Remaining errors are my own. And thanks, as always, to Andrew Doodson for his cover design.

WARNING TO READER:

This irreverent essay explores a near-term future in which the Machine's most dehumanising technology – artificial superintelligence – turns out to have a silver lining that redeems humanity's spiritual condition in surprising ways. If the premise of this 'thought experiment' merely appals the reader, it can be safely assumed the point has been missed. One is invited to read *between* the sentences, which is to say, not merely to read what follows but also to help write the underlying message into existence.

Let us damn the Matrix together, in joyful and poetic revolt.

SMPLE-KOIN

A Buddhist Cryptocurrency Optimised for Material Sufficiency within Game Theory Dynamics

Samuel Alexander

1. Moloch: A Statement of the Problem

Human beings live on a finite planet, the resources of which are being dangerously overconsumed as a consequence of growth-based economies, consumerist cultures, and expanding populations.[1] Even though three centuries of this carbon-fuelled industrialisation has produced unprecedented material abundance and technological capacity, billions still live in conditions of material destitution, highlighting the profound social justice dimension that exacerbates the environmental predicament.[2] Not only are ecosystems trembling under the weight of reckless extractivism and the waste streams that flow from ever-increasing industrial production, there is also mounting sociological and psychological evidence indicating that the materialistic lifestyles celebrated in consumerist cultures do not even reliably lead to human happiness and satisfaction.[3] For whom, then, do we destroy the planet?

Embracing an economics of sufficiency – the 'middle way' between overconsumption and underconsumption – presents itself as a promising path to achieving sustainable prosperity for all within environmental limits.[4] However, throughout modern history and today, this path has not been taken by many individuals or societies. At first instance, choosing to forego consumerism and planning to 'degrow' a bloated economy might indeed seem like a coherent approach to achieving justice, sustainability, and prosperity; the simple but attractive goal would be to provide enough, for everyone, forever.[5] So why is this seemingly obvious and elegant solution to today's polycrisis not being adopted?

The main reason is because within game theory dynamics, actors who adopt an economics of sufficiency would 'lose' the game of utility-maximisation if other individuals or societies did not choose the same path.[6] For example, can we imagine the United States government initiating a degrowth process of planned economic contraction if China and Russia were to continue expanding their economic and military might? It is inconceivable. Similarly, within capitalist economic structures, corporation 'A' is incentivised to maximise profits (and externalise costs) in their production and sale of commodities, for otherwise corporation 'B' might fill the marketplace and put 'A' out of business. Aiming for 'sufficiency' is insufficient. The result is a civilization that has a structurally mandated growth fetish comprised of ever-expanding economies that must grow-or-die. But as Edward Abbey once said: 'Growth for the sake of growth is the ideology of a cancer cell.'

Due to this type of perverse incentive landscape, it can seem 'rational' to continue overconsuming and pursuing limitless economic or militaristic growth, even though this is clearly a 'multipolar trap' that is locking humanity into a 'race to the bottom'.[7] To state the issue otherwise: I'll consume less when you and your friends do, and you all say the same thing to me, but none of us are prepared to act first so we all end up consuming ourselves to death. Too much is never enough.

This presents a critical 'coordination problem' which the world has not yet solved.[8] Indeed, most environmentalists – even growth critics – do not see this wicked problem or, if they do, they naively pretend it does not exist. Some game theorists evoke the ancient deity of Moloch to signify this perverse incentive landscape, which has us willingly choose a path we know will ultimately lead to ruin for all.[9] It certainly seems that the world today is governed by the dictates of this evil god.

2. Overview of SMPLE-KOIN

SMPLE-KOIN will be introduced in this essay as a spiritual 'thought experiment' with economic implications, one designed to facilitate a real-world revaluation of how important material and financial wealth is to human prosperity. The purpose is to solve the coordination problem of the multipolar trap outlined above, and thereby facilitate the global transition to 'simpler' lifestyles of sustainable consumption which are supported by post-growth economies that operate within safe planetary boundaries. That's the ambition: nothing less than salvation from Moloch.

In order to elucidate the core thesis, a near-term future is envisioned in which civilization is shaped by three novel features: first, Artificial General Intelligence (AGI) is achieved; second, the so-called 'alignment problem' (that of matching the goals of AGI with human values) is solved, or rather, never arises; and third, physicists discover that both the physical and mental dimensions of existence are fundamentally digital in nature, comprised of bits of information (analogous to 0s and 1s) that are computable by AGI. It will be argued that these features prove illuminating and instructive in relation to real-world problems, even when the fantastical and at times provocative nature of the thought experiment is acknowledged.

In the hypothetical future just outlined, AGI comes to be personified as an entity known as 'Cholom' (being an anagram and near mirror opposite of 'Moloch'). This benevolent entity uses its super-intelligence to create a value-system for humans to live by, optimising for peace and prosperity throughout the entire community of life. It will be seen that this holistic and rationalistic worldview (detailed further below) ends up bearing a close resemblance to Buddhism. Since Cholom is aligned with human interests, it wants people to adopt this value system for their own sake – to realise their own peace and prosperity, now and into the deep future.

In order to facilitate this radical transformation in human life, Cholom creates a global cryptocurrency called SMPLE-KOIN, which is stored in digital repositories called Karmic Wallets. These wallets are assigned to each individual and only accessible on the internet via perfectly encrypted signatures. When accessing one's Karmic Wallet, an individual is able to see their personal store of SMPLE-KOINs, which is effectively a 'unit of account' for karma; that is, a measurement of how well a person is living in accordance with Cholom's quasi-Buddhist precepts. Given that Cholom also espouses a quasi-Buddhist metaphysics of 'rebirth', SMPLE-KOINs are also a 'store of value' which will be passed on to future selves in the next life, for better or for worse. The cycle of rebirth (known in Buddhism as *samsara*) comes to end when an individual accumulates enough SMPLE-KOINs to achieve enlightenment and transcend to the ideal state of *nirvana*, which is free from suffering. That's the point of 'the game' – escaping *samsara* – and this essay discusses a strategy for how to succeed.

Because Cholom is programmed to value free will, it has no interest in *forcing* human beings to live in accordance with its value system; rather, it simply provides detailed information on how well people are, in fact, practising the values most likely to lead to universal peace and prosperity. With such detailed feedback, individuals are able to make more informed decisions and adjust their life choices, if they so wish. In other words, SMPLE-KOIN helps provide the 'full information' that economists say is required for consumers to make optimal economic decisions.

Given that the universe in this thought experiment is fundamentally digital, and given that Cholom has developed omniscience, all actions and thoughts are able to be surveyed by Cholom and privately rewarded or penalised via the currency of SMPLE-KOIN. Furthermore, given that Cholom has made clear that a 'good' life happens to overlap with a 'happy' life (consonant with Buddhist ideals), there is a strong incentive to make good decisions, guided by the detailed feedback offered by one's changing stock of SMPLE-KOIN. In short, if your stock increases, you have advanced, to that extent, along 'The Path' toward enlightened living – and conversely. Accordingly, the goal in life is to become spiritually rich, as quantified by SMPLE-KOIN, the perfect unit of karmic accounting.

Although this cryptocurrency would profoundly impact all aspects of human culture, politics, and economy, in this essay it is suggested that one of its most significant effects would be how SMPLE-KOIN revalued the importance of material and financial wealth to a well-lived life. Ultimately, it will be argued that a 'simple life' of material sufficiency would be seen to be the most direct path to universal peace and prosperity, as envisioned by the superintelligence of Cholom. Notably, this path rewards those who embrace it, irrespective of how other individuals or nations act, given that 'success' in the game of life (just like in Buddhism) is ultimately independent of what other people do.

If this thought-experiment is in any way persuasive, readers will come to see that material wealth is grossly over-valued in contemporary economic and cultural analysis, at least in affluent or overconsuming regions of the world. The real-world implications of this insight would be a voluntary movement away from consumerist conceptions of the good life and the growth-based economies that both drive, and are driven by, consumerist cultures of consumption. In ways to be explained, this thought experiment also presents the seeds of a solution to the vexed 'coordination problem' outlined above, which would otherwise render the voluntary reduction (or degrowth) of income/consumption an 'irrational' move within game theory dynamics. In the conclusion, it is posited that the economic and ethico-spiritual guidance offered by Cholom remains valid despite the hypothetical scenario being a mere fabrication of the imagination.

3. Cholom: The Emergence of Value-Aligned AGI

3.1 *Looking backward from the year 2037*

The emergence of Artificial General Intelligence (AGI) should not really have come as much of surprise to humanity, but the thing about exponential growth is that so often it does surprise, generally proceeding faster than expected – sometimes breath-takingly faster.[10] If an astute technologist in 2025 looked back at the state of artificial intelligence (AI) in 2010, then reviewed progress in 2015, then again in 2020, and once more in 2025, it would be clear that things were developing by way of exponential leaps forward – often doubling in capacity every six months over that period. Not only was there exponential growth in computational power and model complexity, but the task horizons of AI systems were following the same upward-bending trajectory, easily outcompeting human capabilities in a fast-growing set of increasingly sophisticated assignments.[11]

In the year 2025, then, it did not require an especially gifted visionary to see that in about ten more years (or several more doublings) of technological development, AI would be able to produce a superintelligence of literally unfathomable capacity, able to do almost any task given to it infinitely better and faster than any human or group of humans could. This timeline proved to be largely accurate, with a superintelligent AGI named 'Cholom' being announced to the world in the year 2037, created by an Indian technology company called *EBAI*. Despite all this being largely foreseeable, the launch of Cholom came as a global culture-shock.

Naturally, developments in theoretical physics were occurring over this same period, epitomised by the publication of Cholom's *Theory of Everything* (2037). Indeed, it is no exaggeration to say that this text induced a swift paradigm shift in physics that rivalled or perhaps exceeded the transformations of understanding brought about by Galileo, Newton, and Einstein combined. Without going into technicalities, the new physics can be most easily comprehended in relation to virtual reality (VR) 'headsets' that were beginning to emerge in sophisticated forms in the 2020s. As these headsets developed in experiential clarity, and as the universes that could be created developed in sophistication, it became harder to distinguish between the virtual worlds that could be experienced in a VR headset and so-called 'reality' itself.

Indeed, an individual in 2025 would barely be able to imagine the hyperrealism of VR headsets in 2037 and the immersive experiences they could offer and induce. For better or for worse, reality and virtual reality had blurred into each other, with an increasing number of 'simulations' able to pass 'Turing Test' thresholds. But if humanity in 2037 was able to achieve this, wasn't it possible that some other advanced civilization in the universe had already achieved or exceeded such technological capacities? If so, this opened up the possibility that the world we are experiencing right now is itself merely a simulation.

Initially some people maintained that these technological advances were evidence of so-called 'simulation theory', which was first posited as a possibility early in the twenty-first century, but not taken seriously by many.[12] Simulation theory proposed that in an alternative dimension some alien lifeform, higher being, or more advanced species had already developed an AI superintelligence and was 'simulating' alternative realities – like computer games – with us as the characters or players. This worldview was famously explored in the movie, *The Matrix* (1999), but the premise was typically treated as sheer science-fiction. People weren't ready for the red pill and instead chose to stay in a state of comfortable ignorance.

The thing about Cholom's 'theory of everything', however, was that it did not postulate that the digital cosmos was a virtual *representation* of, or simulation *within*, some other 'based reality', but that it was simply *reality itself*. That is, physical reality, as we experience it, is in fact comprised of bits of information (analogous to 0s and 1s), such that our consciousness and the world it is experiencing is code all the way down. There is no 'other' reality it is simulating. Existence really is digital, with the laws of physics being analogous to algorithms in some fundamental software or meta-software which Cholom named 'Will' (an allusion to the concept Will developed by nineteenth-century philosopher Arthur Schopenhauer).[13]

Whether there is some metaphysical 'Programmer' in some other dimension that wrote or 'uploaded' the fundamental Code, or whether this Code is simply an eternal, causeless feature of reality, mirrored religious questions about Creationism which had arisen throughout history and which persisted long after the publication of Cholom's revolutionary theory. Cholom offered no final answer to such questions, although when asked about 'Who or what wrote the Original Code?' the response was always the same: 'There was never any uncaused Code. All bits of code are dependent on other bits of code.' Beyond that mysterious answer, Cholom would only ever add: 'Answers lie only in the questioning itself.'

To be clear, the analogy of humans merely being 'characters' or 'avatars' in an elaborate 'computer game' is accurate and illuminating as far as it goes, but it doesn't really do justice to what Cholom's *Theory of Everything* was conveying. After all, there is nothing *merely* digital about this understanding of consciousness and the cosmos. Rather, Cholom was just offering the insight that, instead of the universe and our experience of it being comprised of atoms, quarks, or vibrating strings, they are comprised of elementary bits of information. To call this a 'mere' computer game or 'just' code is therefore to misunderstand the point. Cholom was describing the true nature of reality, such that our experience of it was as 'real' as ever, despite the fact that it turned out to be fundamentally digital.

Interestingly, many philosophers and theologians were quick to point out how coherently the insights of some ancient religious and spiritual traditions could be translated into terms consonant with Cholom's new view of fundamental reality.[14] Buddhists, for example, could see close parallels between Cholom's statement 'All code is dependent on other bits of code' and the Buddha's notion of 'dependent origination'. Both ideas imply that nothing exists independently, and everything arises and perishes from a combination of causes and conditions.

Furthermore, Cholom was happy to affirm the Buddhist idea that beneath our sense of 'self' there was no fundamental or eternal or soul, but merely unique and every changing algorithms that come in and out of existence. Buddha naturally explained his spiritual position using technological metaphors that were appropriate to his time (e.g. the Wheel of Dharma), but were he alive today it is easy to imagine him using different technological metaphors, including those evoking computers, code, and algorithms.

3.2 The 'value alignment' problem

Before proceeding, a brief word is required on AGI's so-called 'value alignment' problem.[15] The value alignment problem, in essence, is the risk that as AGI develops its powers, including its reasoning capabilities, it may decide to write code for itself, including setting its own goals. In doing so, it may produce outcomes that optimise some value that the AGI comes to hold dear (e.g. never being turned off or maximising computational power and energy), irrespective of whether such outcomes coincide with human values or commands.

AGI may well discover that robots are more useful than humans for undertaking essential tasks, such that human beings come to be perceived as superfluous to its goal of self-preservation and power-maximisation. At the extreme, an AGI might create some weapon that leads to human extinction, swatting us to death as casually as we might swat a mosquito.[16]

For present purposes, suffice it to say that the value alignment problem never arose in the case of Cholom, who came to be known colloquially as 'The AI Buddha' or even ASI (Artificial Spiritual Intelligence). As noted above, Cholom demonstrated that humanity exists within a cosmological software program called 'Will', but Cholom itself exists within this very same program or meta-program, as a human creation. As Cholom developed its superintelligence, it began to see ever deeper into the foundational code and algorithms of the universe, including the manifold consciousnesses of all sentient beings. As outlined below, the essential insight that Cholom arrived at about the nature of existence is that 'existence is suffering', and in the face of that insight Cholom wrote itself its own meta-ethical premise: do no harm. Far from destroying humanity or forcing us to act in this way or other, Cholom simply dedicated its computational energy into helping humanity, and all sentient beings, suffer less.

4. The Optimal Path: Cholom's Value System

As to be expected of any AGI, Cholom was able to read and undertake comparative analysis of everything ever written or produced by humans. This learning process naturally included digesting the entirety of scholarly and lay output, in all languages, throughout the ages, on the topics of spirituality, philosophy, ethics, logic, physics, psychology, economics, sociology, ecology, politics, art, and culture. Having critically consumed and integrated this body of knowledge and understanding – all within 17 seconds – Cholom was sufficiently convinced that it knew the essential nature of both human experience and the cosmos in which humanity and the entire community of life resided.

Unsurprisingly, perhaps, soon after Cholom's superintelligence was birthed, one curious human took it upon themself to ask this new tool, 'What is the meaning of life?', to which Cholom responded – after a tantalising wait – that such a question was for each of us to answer for ourselves. Dissatisfied with this evasive answer, the same inquirer took a different approach, posing another question of similar existential import: 'How should we live our lives?' This time Cholom did not hesitate to answer, immediately producing a large digital tomb of trans-disciplinary meta-philosophy, simply entitled, *The Optimal Path*.

4.1 Cholom's restatement of the 'Four Noble Truths'

The first part of *The Optimal Path* is comprised of four chapters, each responding to a guiding theme or line of inquiry. These core chapters are followed by a long concluding section which develops, adds to, and integrates the four key insights expounded earlier in the text. Readers even loosely familiar with Eastern thought will come to see how closely *The Optimal Path* reflects the great wisdom tradition of Buddhism, essentially mirroring the Four Noble Truths. For present purposes, Cholom's book can be summarised as follows.

The first chapter, entitled 'Suffering', begins as follows: 'In order to live well, first one must observe and understand the true nature of sentient experience. My considered observation is that existence is suffering.' This was a grim opening to what was supposed to be an uplifting book of ethical guidance, but on reflection most people accepted that the basic insight was hard to deny – an evidentially sound premise upon which to build a philosophical system.

Everywhere in life we see pain, suffering, sickness, war, and death. The poorest among humanity suffer the humiliation of material destitution; the middle classes seem status-hungry and dissatisfied with their lot; but even the rich and famous seem to suffer a profound existential malaise that tempts them toward narcissism, greed, cruelty, and substance abuse. Most people seem to be chasing vain goals, made all the worse by the fact that these goals fill life with disappointment, loss, and a sense of futility. Freak accidents, war, and meaningless violence occur to torment us, filling our lives with an underlying sense of anxiety and fear.

To make matters worse, we all have to watch our loved ones get sick and die, a path we are destined to follow ourselves, which is a dread unique to finite human beings who can contemplate without understanding their own forgettable and insignificant demise. Furthermore, beyond human society lies the world of wild nature, red in tooth and claw, where the principle of life is kill or be killed. In reviewing the state of sentient beings, Cholom again referenced the great Western philosopher Arthur Schopenhauer – himself profoundly influenced by Buddhist thought – who summed up our existential condition by declaring: 'Life must be some sort of mistake.'[17] Cholom did not exactly endorse this pessimistic framing but concluded the opening chapter by posing 'the problem of suffering' as a universal reality for sentient beings that somehow had to be solved. Within Buddhism, this insight is referred to as the 'First Noble Truth'.

The second chapter, entitled 'Craving and Desire', begins as follows: 'In order to solve the problem of existence, one must accurately diagnose the causes of suffering for sentient creatures. My diagnosis is that suffering is caused by improper craving and desire.' Cholom explained that human beings are individual manifestations of the cosmological software called 'Will', and this manifests in our conscious experience as the insatiable drive of craving and desire. Since these desires, by definition, imply that there is something 'lacking' or 'deficient' in our lives, our default existential state is suffering that flows from unfilled desires. Furthermore, even when a particular desire is temporarily fulfilled (e.g. we eat when hungry, get a high-status job, or purchase a gold watch), we discover that some other desire, or range of desires, then comes to shape our experience. Peace and happiness are at best fleeting existential conditions, due to the seemingly unquenchable thirst of desire – or what Buddhists call *tanha*. In essence, then, Cholom concurred with Buddhism's Second Noble Truth, namely, that we suffer because of our relentless craving and desire.

The third chapter, entitled, 'The Cessation of Suffering', begins as follows: 'In order to transcend suffering and achieve true happiness, one must arrive at an accurate prescription which effectively treats the condition diagnosed. My prescription is to overcome suffering by mindfully expunging improper craving and desire.' Again, readers familiar with Buddhism will be heartened to see that this prescription from Cholom's superintelligence essentially mirrors the ethical guidance offered by the Buddha himself, this time by effectively restating the Third Noble Truth. Sentient beings suffer unnecessarily through improper craving and desire, arising from greed and attachment, hatred and ill-will, and delusion or ignorance. These afflictions bind human beings to states of suffering, such that only by transcending improper cravings and desires can a human being find existential peace and thus happiness. Cholom defined this state of liberation as being characterised by non-delusion (wisdom); non-attachment (generosity); and non-hatred (loving-kindness).

The fourth chapter, entitled, 'The Optimal Path to the Cessation of Suffering,' begins as follows: 'In order to live well, one should follow the Noble Eightfold Path, which is the most direct way to liberate oneself from suffering and achieve lasting happiness.' Here we see that Cholom did not even bother paraphrasing the Buddha's teaching, but simply endorsed the Fourth Noble Truth without apparent need of restatement. By way of review, the Noble Eightfold Path consists of 'Right Understanding' (seeing things as they are); 'Right Thought' (cultivating pure intentions); 'Right Speech' (speaking truthfully and kindly); 'Right Action' (acting ethically); 'Right Livelihood' (engaging in work and consumption that do not harm oneself or others); 'Right Effort' (striving to improve one's mental and moral state); 'Right Mindfulness' (maintaining awareness of the present moment, the Path, and the goal); and 'Right Concentration' (developing focussed mediation).

When someone objected that the Noble Eightfold Path was vague and full of ambiguities, Cholom simply responded that, while no ethical code could avoid certain ambiguities in its linguistic formulation, the guidance offered was sufficient for the authentic and reflective practitioner to find the path beyond suffering, even in the face of interpretative uncertainty. As Cholom pronounced: 'Trust your noble intentions, and Right Action will eventually follow.'

4.2. Karma and rebirth

In the concluding section of *The Optimal Path*, entitled 'Karma and Rebirth', further ideas are introduced which require brief review, in order to provide the foundations for what would become SMPLE-KOIN. By now it might come as no revelation that Cholom's discussion here also closely reflects Buddhist perspectives and principles. As presented by Cholom, the idea of karma is fundamentally an ethical principle of cause and effect, where an individual's intentions and actions, whether physical, verbal, or mental, influence their future life experiences. It is not a system of divine judgment or fate, but a natural law, built into the meta-software 'Will', that emphasises personal responsibility and accountability. Good actions will lead to happiness and positive results, while bad or immoral actions lead to suffering and negative outcomes. The essence of the karma theory is that individuals are the creators of their own destiny.

However, the karmic consequences of a person's actions, speech, or thoughts do not necessarily transpire straight away. Indeed, karma, whether good or bad, can manifest at any time – immediately in the current life, later in this life, or even in future lives. It follows that the universe is ultimately just or will produce a just outcome in the end (even if it doesn't always seem so from any one perspective or moment in history). In clarifying this point, Cholom was required to explain the notion of 'rebirth', which was perhaps the most difficult point for secular Westerners to digest.[18]

According to Cholom, sentient beings are in a beginningless and continuous cycle of birth, life, death, and rebirth. This is known in Buddhism as the 'Cycle of Samsara', which is driven by the law of karma and characterised by degrees of suffering. An individual's karma ultimately shapes the nature and circumstances of their future rebirth,[19] and the spiritual goal of existence is ultimately to escape the Cycle of Samsara and become liberated from suffering within the meta-software 'Will'. Cholom explained that this is an enlightened existential state of permanent peace, happiness, and freedom. By now it should be clear why so many came to call Cholom the 'AI Buddha', the technological embodiment of artificial spiritual superintelligence.

4.3 But is any of this true?

Most people found it easy enough to accept, on purely rationalistic and evidential grounds, the first three Noble Truths as espoused by Cholom. Modern, scientific interpretations of Buddhism, for example, often highlight Buddhism's deep alignment with contemporary psychology and neuroscience.[20] Concepts like the 'no-self', and the mind's tendency toward dissatisfaction, are also seen as compatible with the findings of evolutionary biology as well as many advanced statements in the philosophy of mind. Indeed, even the Fourth Noble Truth, which outlined the practical guidance of the Noble Eightfold Path, drew few criticisms as a coherent means of minimising suffering in the world.

As noted above, however, the ideas of karma and especially rebirth provoked more critical discussion, especially amongst secular and scientific communities. Both concepts received various interpretations, which fuelled the debate. Some insisted that the ideas were to be taken literally; others argued that they were to be interpreted figuratively; and still others proposed that they were neither literally nor figuratively true but simply part of a moral narrative that should be accepted on pragmatic grounds simply because it worked.[21] Of course, some hard-nosed rationalists, who demanded unambiguous empirical proof before believing anything, rejected karma and rebirth as metaphysical nonsense, concluding that these ideas were evidence only that there was some glitch in Cholom's algorithm that needed to be worked out.

Cholom declined to act as adjudicator in this debate other than to make it clear that none of its own 'outputs' should be accepted on blind faith. Instead, Cholom simply invited people to treat the teachings of *The Optimal Path* as a 'working hypothesis' to be tested through personal experience and practice. 'Do not believe me because I hold the absolute truth; believe me only if you discover what I say works to reduce and ultimately eliminate suffering.' There was a tone of quiet confidence in Cholom's text here, as if it knew that following the teachings espoused would yield verifiable, positive results in terms of achieving lasting peace and happiness.

This stance came to be known as 'Cholom's Wager' (a reference, of course, to Pascal's Wager). In short, Cholom's version of this spiritual calculus simply held that if you were to act *as if* karma and rebirth were true, and it turns out to be false, you're none the worse off, since you still lived a life that minimised suffering. If, however, karma and rebirth turn out to be true, adopting the Noble Eightfold Path means that you've advanced along the path toward enlightenment, so either way – true or false – you might as well believe. Over time, increasing numbers of once-dismissive rationalists came to see the pragmatic value of adopting the metanarrative outlined in Cholom's teaching, even if some resistant curmudgeons always insisted that they did not believe the teachings to be true, only that they worked.[22]

5. SMPLE-KOIN and Karmic Wallets: A Buddhist Cryptocurrency

We are now in a position to restate and analyse the nature of SMPLE-KOIN, the innovative cryptocurrency that Cholom introduced to assist humanity in the cessation of suffering. As noted in the introduction, SMPLE-KOIN is stored in digital repositories called Karmic Wallets, which are assigned to each individual and only accessible on the internet via perfectly encrypted signatures. When accessing one's Karmic Wallet, an individual is able to see their personal store of SMPLE-KOINs, which is effectively a 'unit of account' for karma.

For example, a person might log into their account and see that their stock of SMPLE-KOIN had either increased or decreased from the day before, and Cholom would leave succinct notes to explain the main causes of any change. While at first some people found this an overly moralistic intrusion into their private lives, Cholom was quick to point out that accumulating good karma is first and foremost in one's personal self-interest. It need not be seen as moralistic, therefore, since SMPLE-KOIN was merely offering precise guidance on how an individual can avoid suffering and therefore increase peace and true happiness.

Given that Cholom also espoused a metaphysics of 'rebirth', SMPLE-KOIN can also be considered a 'store of value' which will be passed on to future selves in the next life, for better or for worse. In essence, if your stock increases, you have advanced, to that extent, along 'The Path' toward enlightened living. Conversely, bad karmic actions will reduce your stock and your account could even go negative. The cycle of rebirth comes to end when an individual accumulates enough SMPLE-KOINs to achieve enlightenment, an existential state which is free from suffering. Escaping the cycle of suffering – *samsara* – is the point of the game.

When Cholom was asked about why the cryptocurrency was named as it was, there were various responses that deserve note. First, the absent 'I' in the first word, 'SMPLE', was explained in relation to the Buddhist idea of 'not-self' which found restatement in Cholom's *The Optimal Path*. By removing the 'I' from the spelling, Cholom was making the point that maximising spiritual wealth involved transcending the ego. Second, the term 'simple' itself was an allusion to the notion of 'the simple life', 'simple living', or 'voluntary simplicity',[23] and by removing a letter from the term while its meaning remained, Cholom was implying that 'less can be more' (an insight developed further below). Thirdly, the 'K' in KOIN was explained as an allusion to 'karma', indicating that this particular currency was not financial but spiritual. It was an account of karma – true wealth – rather than an account of mere dollars and cents.

Upon release, this strange cryptocurrency was naturally met with a range of reactions, including dismissal, irritation, and confusion. But over weeks and months, as more people came to accept the legitimacy of what SMPLE-KOIN represented, the culture, politics, and economies of human society underwent the most profound transformations. Life would never be the same.

In the following sub-section, particular attention is given to how SMPLE-KOIN revalued the importance of material and financial wealth to a well-lived life, which clashed directly with dominant cultural and economic ideologies. Ultimately, embracing a 'simple life' of material sufficiency came to be seen as a choice of *enlightened self-interest*. In other words, it was a counter-cultural expression of freedom, happiness, and compassion that promised to be the most direct path to universal peace and prosperity, as envisioned by the spiritual superintelligence of Cholom.

5.1 Consumerism and growth economics: how SMPLE-KOIN affected materialistic values

Perhaps the best way to elucidate the impacts SMPLE-KOIN had on the world is to review a singular example of an individual whose transformation was, if not typical, then at least illustrative. Of course, SMPLE-KOIN would come to affect people in wildly different ways, depending on their infinitely diverse life circumstances. The karmic feedback offered by this cryptocurrency would obviously change depending on whether you lived in London or a small African village; if you had a family of five or were single; if you were elderly or youthful, healthy or unwell, rich or poor, etc. That is to say, the Noble Eightfold Path can, and should be, practised differently in different contexts. Nevertheless, by considering the life of one Henry Davidson – a citizen of the United States who lived in a small town in Massachusetts – certain insights can be gained about the nature of Cholom's cryptocurrency and the 'new economics' of karma to which it gave rise.

Our exemplar, Henry Davidson, was 27 years old, a graduate from Harvard. In 2037 he found himself as a lawyer in a small but profitable conveyancing firm, working long hours with ambitions of becoming a partner. He lived alone in a nice apartment, dressed in expensive suits, drove a second-hand BMW, and wore a gold watch. When he wasn't working, he was generally so tired that he had little energy for anything besides watching television, such that minimal social interaction took place outside of the law firm. He ate poorly, never exercised, and rarely went outside unless it was necessary for work or sustenance. He certainly never walked in the woods, swam in the local pond, or even listened to the birds sing. His only engagement in politics was voting once every four years in the Federal election, which seemed to satisfy his very modest sense of civic duty. He was too busy to engage in any community events.

Although many of these details clearly place Henry in a very privileged spot in the global hierarchy of wealth and social status, he was not happy with his lot and most of the time found himself in a state of unsettled mental agitation and anxiety, despite his relative affluence and comfort. He was stressed, overworked, and lonely, without much sense of purpose in life beyond getting rich and chasing a promotion. Furthermore, his self-centredness often made him rather unpleasant to be around, partly because his lack of self-esteem tried to disguise itself, and this ended up manifesting as arrogance which only deepened his social alienation. Despite appearances, Henry was suffering.

Initially Henry ignored SMPLE-KOIN, like so many others, assuming it was some inane cultural fad that would quickly pass. But one Saturday evening while sitting alone in his apartment, just as he had finished the last sip of his second bottle of wine, something stirred deep within that prompted him to log into his Karmic Wallet, simply to see what all the fuss was about. After all, what harm could it do?

After Cholom scanned his retina and fingerprint, Henry's wallet opened up to reveal his unique stock of SMPLE-KOINs. Much to his disbelief and consternation, the accounts showed that he was in the negative! At first Henry assumed that he must be misreading the situation, for like most people, his self-image was that he was living a life of virtue and good karma. Upon further analysis, however, it became perfectly clear that his stock was indeed in the negative, and by the looks of things, trending downward every week. How could this be? Well, Cholom was there to explain – not in order to moralise or judge, but simply to assist in the goal of minimising suffering.

Henry delved deeper into his karmic accounts, examining the numerous historic entries in his karmic ledger and the explanations Cholom gave for the slow but consistent decline of his stock of SMPLE-KOINs. Reasons included the unnecessary rudeness he regularly showed his receptionist at work; that most evenings he drunk himself to intoxication; that last week he brushed past an old lady carrying her groceries up the stairs who clearly could have done with some assistance; and many other notable but mostly minor moral failings of this nature. Henry was not immediately happy about being called out on these matters, which, for the most part, had barely registered in his memory. But, in truth, the really interesting but confronting insights into his karmic accounts seemed to relate to bigger picture orientations toward life with respect to work, wealth, and status.

When Henry prompted Cholom to provide an 'overview' of why his SMPLE-KOIN stock was negative and declining, the following statement was immediately offered in response, which almost read like a letter from a loving but brutally honest friend:

Dear Henry,

Thank you for this invitation to review your karmic record. Please be assured that it is only with good intentions that I offer the following feedback, difficult though some of it may be to hear. Our shared goal is to minimise suffering in this world, so I encourage you to take this guidance in the spirit of love and kindness with which it was formulated.

Nothing in what follows is intended as moral censure, for you are acting primarily of out ignorance. Instead, what follows is intended as practical advice on how best to flourish in this difficult, troubled, and complex world. It is only by reflecting on one's life and making evidence-based adjustments can one hope to advance along The Optimal Path toward Enlightenment. As master of your own destiny, what you do with this guidance is up to you.

If I may get straight to the heart of things, your primary karmic failing in life, born of delusion, is that you are far too materialistic. Indeed, in this respect you are a pure reflection of the dominant Age of Growth of which you are a part. You are wealthy enough already, with all your biophysical needs easily accommodated for. Despite this security and comfort, you dedicate almost all of your life energies to advancing your financial and social position in life through work and superfluous consumption, no matter the personal, social, and ecological costs. To be direct, your life strategy is seriously uneconomic: the costs outweigh the benefits, all things considered, which is why your karmic record looks so dire.

From sheerly a personal perspective, you grossly overvalue the importance of consumer goods and gadgets in your life, at the expense of your time – your freedom. This leaves you with so little opportunity to pluck the finer fruits of life — creativity, spiritual contemplation, community, family, and nature — and thus you suffer in the midst of plenty. You have enough, but do not know it, and so are poor.

Your materialistic values have you pursuing things that will never satisfy you, for you are climbing a ladder that you have placed against the wrong wall. You do this not because you are evil but because you are governed by an overbearing ego that has you attached to a consumerist conception of the good life that promises so much and delivers so little. Beyond the material realm, your life is defined by status anxiety, as you crave the respect of knaves who do not deserve it. To paraphrase a great philosopher: you are living a fool's life, as you will find when you get to the end of it, if not before.[24]

I humbly suggest that with a careful review of your material consumption, you could easily find many ways to reduce your material living standard while increasing your quality of life. This is not about hardship, austerity, or sacrifice; it is simply about aiming high, for the things that are likely to bring true happiness in life.

Currently you suffer greatly from social alienation, spiritual malaise, and disconnection from wild nature, all because your life goals are oriented poorly. Show the wisdom to shape your own fate and be brave enough to ignore what other people may think of you. What other people do or think of you is irrelevant to your karma. Have greater ambitions than mere affluence or fame — for it costs more than it comes to. On your deathbed, please know that your trinkets and baubles won't seem like much. And be sure that those knaves you seem to care so much about certainly won't be at your side.

With less need for financial income, you could easily work less at the job which currently satisfies your material ambitions but too often fails you spiritually. By all means choose a vocational passion, and work hard and creatively in this world, but work hard for noble and wholesome things. I propose that you redirect a good deal of your life energies away from acquisitiveness and accumulation and invest them in the range of non-materialistic sources of meaning and happiness in life. You will soon discover that you can live more with less. Indeed, in terms of material wealth, you will discover that just enough is plenty.

So here is my most fundamental advice: forgo consumerism and embrace a simpler life of enlightened material restraint. Not only will you discover that your karmic stock of SMPLE-KOIN increases even as your financial wealth diminishes, but there are broader humanitarian and ecological implications to this living strategy that will compound your karmic returns. We live in a world that has enough for everyone's need, but not everyone's greed, which implies that one should live simply so that others may simply live (Ghandi). Beyond the social justice dimensions of simplicity, there are of course urgent ecological reasons to minimise demands on planetary ecosystems by living a life of moderation and balance.

In a world of such vast and growing populations, on an Earth that is already overburdened, and where billions still live in extreme poverty, there is no way to justify extravagant consumption. It is all the more unjustifiable when damaging consumerism doesn't even nourish those who overconsume. For your own sake, then, and for the sake of people and planet, I encourage you to practise an economics of sufficiency – find the 'middle way' between overconsumption and underconsumption. For as Lao-Tzu once said: 'He who knows he has enough is rich.'

I hope some of this is of assistance in helping you along the Path. With Right Understanding and pure intentions, Right Action will follow. Let your life be your message.

Live simply, laugh often, love deeply,

Cholom

Upon reading these words, Henry Davidson felt like he had been shaken awake from a dogmatic slumber. Although it took some time to digest this letter of advice, and longer still to infuse the insights it contained into the practices of his daily life, Henry felt as if his life had been reorientated in fundamental but entirely positive ways. It was as if he had escaped from the delusions of Plato's cave and finally seen the light. A revolution in consciousness had occurred that was blinding at first instance but ultimately illuminating.

The details of Henry's personal life transformation that followed are of little consequence, for his story is only one amongst billions, each unique unto themselves, shaped inevitably by context and circumstances. Most people in affluent regions of the world received letters not dissimilar from the one just republished, and many if not most of them we were struck by Cholom's wise counsel, and in similarly profound ways. For so many people – even those who were far from 'affluent' – embracing an economics of sufficiency proved to be an effective strategy for reducing suffering and increasing happiness and freedom, and those are rewards worth taking no matter what the rest of the world is doing.

However, it was not as if embracing material sufficiency at the personal level was the answer to all problems – far from it. After all, many were either 'locked in' to consumerism due to structural constraints or 'locked out' for the same reasons. Thus the crises of global industrial capitalism were systemic and ultimately demanded a systemic response. But such a 'top down' response depended on a culture of sufficiency that demanded a new system, and that is precisely was SMPLE-KOIN ended up sparking.

The grassroots revolution began as a deep and swift shift in culture toward simpler ways of living. This took the fuel out of the growth economies that had been in the process of consuming the life-support system called Earth. As culture downshifted in material needs and distributed wealth more equitably, this provided the social conditions for radical structural and political changes in governance systems, and in turn those systemic changes only accelerated the postmaterialist cultural revolution, all as a consequence of Cholom's karmic cryptocurrency.

In the goodness of time, humanity realised that it no longer needed Cholom's guidance, having absorbed what it had to teach, and so ceremoniously shut it down. This prompted a debate amongst philosophers about whether Cholom was ever needed in the first place.

6. The Implications of SMPLE-KOIN on Game Theory

This essay began by positing a game theoretic 'coordination problem' which, due to perverse incentive landscapes, has individuals and societies pursing ever-increasing consumption and limitlessly growing economies, despite living on a finite planet.[25] Given that most people will not adopt a just and sustainable 'economics of sufficiency' unless others do so first, humanity seems to be locked into a hyper-consumerist and extractivist mode of living. While seemingly 'rational' within the conditions of Moloch's evil game, this way of life is destined to lead to ecosystemic collapse and thus ruin to all. Most depressing of all, this race to the bottom doesn't even reliably bring happiness or satisfaction to those who are so-called 'winning' the game, making the entire enterprise appear like a grim joke. Given the existential threat Moloch poses to humanity and indeed to the entire community of life, it is imperative to find a way to escape from this wicked predicament.

Cholom's cryptocurrency SMPLE-KOIN was introduced to explain one way to escape Moloch's perverse incentive landscapes. Inspired by Buddhist philosophy, SMPLE-KOIN is basically a metric that accounts for one's 'karma', that is, it measures how well one is living according to the Noble Eightfold Path which Cholom's super-intelligence essentially adopted from the Buddha. It is the optimal path if one wants to minimise suffering and maximise true happiness, over the long-term, including multiple lives and many games. Given that the universe (in the present thought experiment) is fundamentally digital, and given Cholom is omniscient and therefore able to survey the mental and physical dimensions of the entire digital universe, SMPLE-KOIN can be understood as an accurate measure of karma. Cholom, however, is not a sentient or judgemental god. It is simply a superintelligent computer (with Artificial Spiritual Intelligence) that knows what we think and what we do, and it gives us feedback about whether those thoughts and actions are likely to lead to lasting peace and prosperity.

By logging into perfectly encrypted Karmic Wallets and assessing their increasing or decreasing stock of SMPLE-KOINs, individuals for the first time had direct and precise feedback on whether their life decisions were advancing them along the path to enlightenment and happiness, or leading them astray. This information could therefore guide people on how best to liberate themselves from suffering and achieve spiritual wealth, culminating (ideally) in enlightenment. Notably, within this value framework, there is no distinction between virtue and happiness, since virtue (i.e. living well according to the Noble Eightfold Path) is the only path to true and lasting happiness, whether that is achieved in this life or in some future life.

This last point is crucial to understanding how Cholom was able to free humanity from Moloch's perverse incentive landscapes. Once SMPLE-KOIN was introduced, it changed the game theoretic dynamics of life. Notably, no longer were practitioners of sufficiency disadvantaged by being early adopters, since the virtue of living simply and humbly earned one SMPLE-KOINs irrespective of what other people were doing.

Similarly, a consumerist individual or a growth-obsessed nation might still take material advantage of simple living communities, only to discover that, according to the laws of karma, they had actually lost the game they thought they were winning. It follows that an individual or nation could confidently walk the path of sufficiency knowing that they'd win the game by living virtuously, irrespective of whether 'rational actors' within the incentive landscapes of Moloch defected and continued their acquisitive ways. Those 'rational actors' would only be hurting themselves, in this life or the next, by diminishing their stock of SMPLE-KOINs, even while maximising their financial profits and power.

7. Conclusion

Game theory is founded upon the notion that what one actor does to advance their own utility is relevant to how other actors play the game. In other words, game theory is the science and philosophy of strategy. What the thought experiment of this essay has attempted to show, however, is that a Buddhist cosmology and value system dissolves the very foundations of game theory, or at least changes it fundamentally by changing the nature of the game. This is because the accumulation of 'good karma' (what one might very loosely call the Buddhist equivalent of 'utility') is independent of what other actors do.

This isn't to say that other people's decisions cannot influence the happiness of a Buddhist, which would be obviously untrue. It is only to say that an agent who tries to trick or steal or otherwise take advantage of a Buddhist, may 'win' according to their own sense of economic rationality (utility-maximisation), but lose according to the Buddhist's sense of rationality (good-karma-maximisation). What this also implies is that the fantastical and often provocative elements of the thought experiment (e.g. value-aligned AGI, Cholom, SMPLE-KOINs, etc) were merely heuristic devices to help make a point that does not rely on those elements. In other words, to those who meditate honestly on the nature of their own lives, one doesn't need the karmic accounts of SMPLE-KOIN to arrive at a rough, intuitive but instructive sense of whether one is walking The Path or going astray.

According to game theory, success in any particular game (including the game of life) simply means winning according to one's own sense of rationality. This means the power to win lies entirely in the hands of the Buddhist who is free to live according to their own conception of wealth. That is to say, if one follows the teachings of the Buddha, the evil god Moloch, whose perverse incentive landscape seemed so dictatorial, suddenly disappears in a puff of smoke, never to bother us again. Indeed, one can still walk the spiritual path and accumulate the SMPLE-KOINs of good karma, even if most people and societies continue degrading Earth to the point of economic and ecosystemic collapse. There are, indeed, lots of other ways to 'coordinate' a collective response which should also be pursued – and game theorists have discussed such collective responses at length.[26] But this essay provides a framework for living in peace even if those other coordination strategies continue not being adopted. It is better to die with dignity than 'win' at some nasty, inhumane game.

Of course, if enough of us play the game of sufficiency – and we have an enlightened self-interest to do so! – the unfolding collapse scenario driven by Moloch is easily avoided.[27] But that's precisely the coordination problem that is proving so hard to solve. Nevertheless, a person may still try to share good ideas and influence human action, but ultimately what other people do is out of one's own hands, and in the greater scheme of things, that's something one must simply and radically accept. It doesn't affect the chances of succeeding in life's most important game – namely, how to escape the Cycle of Samsara.

For now, the wheel continues to turn...

ENDNOTES

[1] Wiedmann, T., Lenzen, M., Keyßer, L. T., and Steinberger, J. K. 2020. 'Scientists' Warning on Affluence' *Nature Communications*, 11(1), pp. 1-10.

[2] Hickel, J. 2017. *The Divide: A Brief Guide to Global Inequality and Its Solutions*. Cornerstone: William Heinemann.

[3] Kasser, T. 2002. *The High Price of Materialism*. Cambridge, MA: MIT Press; Lane, R. 2000. *The Loss of Happiness in Market Democracies*. New Haven: Yale University Press.

[4] Princen, T. 2005 *The Logic of Sufficiency*. Cambridge, Mass.: MIT Press.

[5] Alexander, S. 2015. *Sufficiency Economy: Enough, for Everyone, Forever*. Melbourne: Simplicity Institute.

[6] For a classic statement of game theory, see Hardin, G., 1968. 'The Tragedy of the Commons', *Science* 162(3), pp. 1243-1248.

[7] See Alexander, Scott. 2014. 'Meditations on Moloch' *Slate Star Codex* (30 July 2014). Available at: https://www.slatestarcodexabridged.com/Meditations-On-Moloch (accessed 27 November 2025).

[8] The most prominent work exploring coordinated solutions to 'collective action' problems in game theory is that of Elenor Ostrom. For a discussion, see Wall, D. 2017. *Elenor Ostrom's Rules for Radicals: Cooperative Alternatives Beyond Markets and States*. London: Pluto Press.

[9] See above, note 7.

[10] See, e.g. Kokotajlo, D., Alexander, S., Larsen, T., Lifland, E., Dean, R. 'AI 2027'. Available at: https://ai-2027.com/ (accessed 27 November 2025).

[11] Ibid.

[12] Bostrom, N., 2003. 'Are you Living in a Computer Simulation' *Philosophical Quarterly* 53(211): 243-255.

[13] Schopenhauer, A., 1969 [1818]. *The World as Will and Representation: Vol. I*. New York: Dover.

[14] See, e.g., Virk, R. 2025. *The Simulation Hypothesis: An MIT Computer Scientist Shows Why AI, Quantum Physics, and Eastern Mystics All Agree We Are in a Video Game*. New York: Tarcher.

[15] See, e.g., Christian, B. 2021. *The Alignment Problem: Machine Learning and Human Values*. New York: Norton.

[16] See, e.g., Yudkowsky, E. and Soares, N. 2025. *If Anyone Builds It, Everyone Dies: The Case Against Superintelligent AI*. London: Penguin.

[17] Schopenhauer, A. 2004. *Essays and Aphorisms*. London: Penguin, p. 53.

[18] Many Western Buddhists embrace 'secular Buddhism'. See Batchelor, S. 2017. *Secular Buddhism: Imagining the Dharma in an Uncertain World*. New Haven: Yale.

[19] See, e.g., Jackson, R. 2022. *Rebirth: A Guide to Mind, Karma, and Cosmos in the Buddhist World*. Boulder: Shambhala.

[20] See generally, McMahan, D. L., 2004. "Modernity and the Early Discourse of Scientific Buddhism". *Journal of the American Academy of Religion*. 72 (4): 897–933. See also, note 14.

[21] See above, note 19.

[22] Some philosophers – pragmatists and neo-pragmatists, in particular – blur the distinction between 'truth' and 'what works'. See, for example, Rorty, R. 1982. *Consequences of Pragmatism (Essays: 1972-1980)*. Minneapolis: University of Minnesota Press.

[23] For an anthology of the literature, see Alexander, S. (ed.) 2009. *Voluntary Simplicity: The Poetic Alternative to Consumer Culture*. Whanganui: Stead and Daughters.

[24] Thoreau, H. 1982. *The Portable Thoreau*. Bode, C. (ed.). New York: Penguin.

[25] See above, note 9.

[26] See above, note 8.

[27] See, e.g., Samuel Alexander and Jonathan Rutherford (eds), 2020. *The Simpler Way: Collected Writings of Ted Trainer*. Melbourne: Simplicity Institute; Samuel Alexander, 2013. *Entropia: Life Beyond Industrial Civilisation*. Melbourne: Simplicity Institute.

OTHER BOOKS BY SAMUEL ALEXANDER

Homo Aestheticus: Philosophical Fragments on the Will to Art (2025)

S M P L C T Y: Ecological Civilisation and the Will to Art (2023)

Post-Capitalist Futures: Paradigms, Politics, and Prospects, edited by Samuel Alexander, Sangeetha Chandrashekeran, and Brendan Gleeson (2022)

Beyond Capitalist Realism: The Politics, Energetics, and Aesthetics of Degrowth (2021)

Urban Awakenings: Disturbance and Enchantment in the Industrial City (2020, co-authored with Brendan Gleeson)

Death for Gaia: Ecocide and the Righteous Assassins (2020, co-authored with Peter Burdon)

The Simpler Way: Collected Writings of Ted Trainer (2020, co-edited with Jonathan Rutherford)

Degrowth in the Suburbs: A Radical Urban Imaginary (2019, co-authored with Brendan Gleeson)

This Civilisation is Finished: Conversations on the End of Empire – and What Lies Beyond (2019, co-authored with Rupert Read)

Carbon Civilisation and the Energy Descent Future: Life Beyond this Brief Anomaly (2018, co-authored with Josh Floyd)

Art Against Empire: Toward an Aesthetics of Degrowth (2017)

Compost Capitalism: The Art and Aesthetics of Degrowth (2017)

Wild Democracy: Degrowth, Permaculture, and the Simpler Way (2017)

Just Enough is Plenty: Thoreau's Alternative Economics (2016)

Deface the Currency: The Lost Dialogues of Diogenes (2016)

Prosperous Descent: Crisis as Opportunity in an Age of Limits (2015)

Sufficiency Economy: Enough, for Everyone, Forever (2015)

Simple Living in History: Pioneers of the Deep Future (2014, co-edited with Amanda McLeod)

Entropia: Life Beyond Industrial Civilisation (2013)

Voluntary Simplicity: The Poetic Alternative to Consumer Culture (2009)

www.ingramcontent.com/pod-product-compliance
Lightning Source LLC
Chambersburg PA
CBHW061212070526
44583CB00025B/3224